Baby
Animals

Written by Emily Bone

Illustrated by Lucye Rioland

Designed by Zoe Wray

Reading consultant: Alison Kelly

Most baby animals are born without any fur.

Baby rabbits are called kits.

Some baby animals are born with lots of fur.

This is a seal and her pup.

Mother animals make milk for their babies to drink.

These are wolf pups.

4

Some babies drink milk and also eat the same things as their parents.

Zebra foals eat grass.

Snow monkey babies eat berries.

High up in a tree, a squirrel collects twigs and leaves.

She uses them to build a nest.

The nest is warm.
Babies are born inside it.

Polar bears are born in a den under the snow.

At the start of winter, a mother polar bear digs the den.

Her cubs are born inside the den.

In the spring, the mother and
cubs will go outside.

Meerkats live in burrows.
Baby meerkats are
called pups.

During the day, meerkats go
out to find food.

A lookout sees danger. He barks.

The meerkats run into the burrow
to stay safe.

Some mothers carry their babies.

A chimpanzee cradles
her baby in her arms.

A tiger carries her
cub in her mouth.

A sloth baby rests on
its mother's tummy.

A kangaroo joey stays
in its mother's pouch.

Giraffe calves are born on grassland in Africa.

A calf can't walk when it's born.

In a few hours, its legs grow stronger.
It can run along with the herd.

Emperor penguins
live in Antarctica.
It is very cold there.

Chicks stay close
to their parents
to keep warm.

In a snow storm, penguins huddle together in a group.

Lion cubs grow up in a group
called a pride.

A lion and a lioness look after the
cubs. The cubs play with each other.

18

Other lions in the pride
hunt for food. They bring
it back for the cubs to eat.

Birds build nests.
They lay eggs in the nest.

Chicks hatch out of the eggs.

Young chicks have no feathers.
They can't fly.

Parents bring food
to the chicks.

Snakes and lizards come from eggs, too. They can look after themselves as soon as they hatch.

Snakes

Lizards

Sharks lay eggs
in the sea.

Shark pups hatch
out of the eggs
and swim away.

Turtles live in the sea. They come onto a beach to lay eggs.

They bury their eggs in the sand.

Baby turtles hatch
out. They dig their
way out of the sand,
then crawl to the sea.

A caterpillar hatches out of an egg.

It eats lots
of leaves.

It grows bigger and bigger.

The caterpillar's skin
turns into a hard
case. Then it
becomes a butterfly.

A frog lays lots of eggs.

Tadpoles grow inside
the eggs. Then the
tadpoles hatch out.

The tadpoles grow legs. Their tails fall off. Then they turn into frogs.

Elephants grow up in a
group called a herd.

There are old and young elephants
in a herd. A baby elephant is
called a calf.

The oldest elephants help the calves
and make sure they stay safe.

Baby animals grow up. Then they have babies of their own.

Digital retouching by John Russell

First published in 2015 by Usborne Publishing Ltd., Usborne House, 83-85 Saffron Hill, London EC1N 8RT England. www.usborne.com Copyright © 2015 Usborne Publishing Ltd. The name Usborne and the devices ♀⊕ are Trade Marks of Usborne Publishing Ltd. All rights reserved.